The Sweet Fragrance

OF

LOVE

Birister Sharma

Dedicated to my loving wife....

Pallabi Devi Sharma

I surrendered to you, O my Lord......

"Om Namah Shivaya"

Table of Contents

One Word

Love is the food of our heart, mind and soul. Love is breath of our life. Without love our life is death or lifeless or meaningless or worthless. We can't think or imagine anything without love.

It is only love which gives us new meaning of our life. It is only love which teaches us the purpose of our life.

Love is the foundation of every relationship. Without love no relationships ever survive in this world.

Love is the mother of everything in this world. Love is the only medicine which heals every wound of our life. We can state that love is the herb of our life.

Without love every creature will die in this world. Love is the only source of life in this entire world. Love is the life saving energy of every creature; love is the only power which combines and binds everything in one knot of togetherness. Love brings everything under one roof or in oneness.

Love is like air we breathe. Love is like water we drink. Love is like fire we get warm. Love is like earth where we live. Love is like the sky which is above us. Love is the element of our life.

Love yourself.

Love your life.

Love your world.

Love your beloved ones.

Love your friends.

Love your neighbors.

Love every creature of this world.

Love is the only way to live in this world with happiness and peace.

It is only love which will change your life.

It is only love which will change your world.

Only love can change you.

Only love can change your life.

Only love can change your world.

---***---

~~***~~

Love is the only way to live in this world with happiness and peace.

~~***~~

1. *Love is beautiful*

Love is the only word which is the most beautiful thing in the whole world or universe. There is no match or any comparison with any other word. It is so beautiful and sweet that everybody can feel it or understand it clearly and wholly. There is not an iota of any doubt that he or she won't feel its beauty and melodious language.

Love is only a word of four letters L-O-V-E, but you won't define it in one word. It's so vast and wide that you won't measure its length. Its meaning is deep and sacred. It is infinite. But it could touch every heart whether man or beast or birds or tress.

Love is the language of universe.

There is a great magic in love. It can mesmerize anybody or anything in this world. Love is only a magic lamp which enlightens your life.

If you want to test its magic then try to express your feelings to your beloved ones or dear ones, say, "I love you, dear." Then you'll see its magical charms. It can melt everybody's heart, mind and soul.

How many times do you express 'I love you, dear' to your beloved ones or dear ones in your life?

Not yet!

Then, try it, if you wish to feel the beauty and magic of love in your life.

'I love you,' is the most beautiful sentence in the entire world. Always keep this beautiful sentence with you like your most valuable treasure wherever you live or wherever you go in your life. This simple sentence will change your life utterly.

Love is the only remedy of every malady of human emotions and feelings.

Feel it!

Express it!

Love is your most valuable treasure.

Live your life with love.

You'll know the real meaning of your life.

Love is the only water which would wet the burning fire of hatred. Love is the only thing which would melt every heart. Love is the only answer of every question of life. Love is the only solution of every problem of life. Love is the only weapon to win any battle of your life.

If you want to bring lasting happiness, success and peace in your life, then start loving your beloved ones or dear ones. Love will definitely fulfill your every wish and every desire of your life. Because love is the ultimate source of your life and your world.

It is only love which always motivates you to live your life.

It is only love which always guides you towards your goals of life.

No love, no motivation in your life.

No love, no guidance in your life.

Without love, you'll lose in your life.

Without love, you'll wander in your world.

Love is the only pathfinder of your life.

But, unfortunately, in today's busy and fast running, and preoccupied world, everybody is, gradually, forgetting this beautiful word 'LOVE'. They have no time to feel or express this beautiful word of love with each other. As a result, in today's materialist world many people's life is becoming a void and hollow. Like a machine. There is always lack of love, lack of happiness and lack of peace, and their lives are engulfing with the darkness of anxieties and stresses.

Everybody is running after name, fame, money, and power, so there is no space for love in their lives. Love becomes secondary stuff for them. They are living with wrong beliefs and wrong notions that if they have named, fame, money, and power, then they would achieve everything in their lives.

Is it really happened in life?

But, alas, when they achieve name, fame, money and power, they lost the most important thing of their lives, which is love. They forget to live their lives.

Without love you'll forget to live your life.

Love is a beauty of this world. Nobody can live without its sweet nectar. If there is love there is life, if there is no love there is no life.

Many people try to seek love elsewhere or in far of distance, instead of finding it within their hearts, and within their beloved ones or dear ones. So they are always unhappy and unsatisfied in their lives no matter how much they are successful in their lives.

In the Himalayan region, a very famous Kasturi male deer is found. It is very beautiful, and it wears black and brown color. Every year, during one of the seasons, a persistent perfume like odor is developed from one of its glands in its navel area which is called kasturi. But the poor deer always remained unaware of it. When it smells its own sweet odor (Kasturi), it becomes so entrapped in its own odor that it starts searching it everywhere, madly. Alas, the poor beast couldn't find it anywhere.

In the same way, many people started seeking their love elsewhere while forgetting that the very thing which they are seeking desperately is much closer to them, in their hearts and in their beloved ones or dear ones.

Love is always dwelling within you.

You just need to realize it.

 Don't look it elsewhere.

You'll never find it anywhere.

Generally, the most common error people commit in their lives is that they are always attracted to the person's beautiful appearances or outlooks, but they are always failed to look at the person's hidden beautiful love and beautiful heart. They will only realize their grave errs when that beautiful appearance wearing person betrays them.

A beautiful love is always dwelling in the heart of a beautiful heart.

A person's appearance may be disappeared or wither one day. His body will get wrinkles one day, and become old and aged with the tides of time, but his beautiful love will ever remain fresh and eternal even after many years.

Love is so beautiful that once you'll fall in love with yourself or with your beloved ones or dear ones, you too automatically become beautiful. Your life will become beautiful. Your world will become beautiful. Everything becomes beautiful. You'll see beautiful in everyone. You'll feel beautiful in everything. You'll find beauty in everywhere.

If you want to make yourself beautiful, then first of all you should love yourself. Only love can make you one of the most beautiful persons in the whole world.

Love makes your heart beautiful.

Love makes your mind beautiful.

Love makes your soul beautiful.

Love makes your thoughts beautiful.

Love makes your life beautiful.

Love makes your world beautiful.

Love makes you a complete man.

Love is the only source of life that changes you completely.

If you want to change yourself or anybody, then it is one and only your love which would spell its beautiful magic, and instantly change you completely.

Love is the only way to change your life in this world.

___***___

Love is beautiful;
it's a beauty of one's heart.
Love is the breath of one's life,
it's a part of one's life.
Love is the rhythm of this world.
Without its sweetness this world will be vacuumed.
Love is love;
nothing will replace its worth.
Love is like a flower,
blooming in everybody's heart.
Without its fragrance one's life is worthless.
Live the life of love,
And spreads its sweet smile everywhere,
So that every heart could smile forever.

---***---

Great thoughts to ponder:

Things are beautiful if you love them.

---Jean Anouilh

That which is love is always beautiful.

---Norwegian proverb

Since love grows within you, so beauty grows for love is the beauty of the soul.

---Saint Augustine

Beauty is simply seen reality with the eyes of love.

---Evelyn Underhill

Love is the most beautiful and rare things there is and, sometimes, you have to be a little bit patient and endure a little bit of pain to reach it.

Love is cute when it's new, but it's most beautiful when it lasts.

12

___***___

~~***~~

Love is the only remedy of every malady of human emotions and feelings.

~~***~~

2. *Love is the mother of everything*

In an Island, once there lived mother Love and her children very happily. The names of her children were: Compassion, Kindness, Mercy, Happiness, Wealth, Unity and Peace.

Mother Love loved her children very much, and her children too loved her dearly. They were always together, and contented with their lives. Wherever mother Love went, her children too followed her.

Hence, there were no such things like hatred, envy, misery, sadness, poverty, disunity and disturbance in the Island. There was complete happiness and lasting peace in the Island. The Island was growing very prosperous, and became very famous tourist destination in the world.

Then as time elapsed, the Island grew haughty and self-centered. He started troubling and ignoring mother Love. And he started giving more importance to her children. When mother Love learned everything, she became very upset, and decided to leave the Island as soon as possible.

Then, one dark night mother Love quietly left the Island forever without informing anybody. The very next day when her children didn't find their doting mother; they too left the Island in search of their mother.

And as soon as mother Love and her children left the Island, the Island turned into a place of chaos and disturbances. Then, there were no more tourists or any visitor ever landed on that Island. And very soon the Island was submerged into the sea.

You're like an Island. Everything is depended upon you, what do you want and what you don't want in your life. When you care love and embrace her in your life, she too embraces you forever in your life. And your world of Island will fill with Compassion, Kindness, Mercy, Happiness, Wealth, Unity and Peace.

In every happy family or good relationship, love is the only key factor to sustain the unity and everlasting bond of relation. Without love there is no family. Without love there is no relationship.

In other words, love is the only foundation of every happy family or good relationship. Only love can cement the concrete mortar of relationships in your life.

Love is the mother of everything. When she put her footsteps in your life, then everything will be followed in your world.

Think for a second, what would be happened in your life if you've no mother. Can you grow up in your life the way you are right today?

No!

You never grow up what you're today. You never become what you're right now. You'll become an orphan. You'll have to grow up without your mother's love. You'll always miss your mother's love throughout your life. And nobody will ever fulfill you your mother's love.

Mother's love is always pure, selfless and unconditional. She never demands anything from her son. Her love is always immortal. She always gives her son whatever she has. Even she is ready to sacrifice her life for her son. She cares her son more than her life.

Even she is ready to jump into the burning house to rescue her child.

However, it is very sad to state that when a mother becomes old, and when her son grows up, her son leave her forever forgetting her every love and sacrifice. There are many such incidents happening around us every day.

Love your mother like you love yourself.

If you love your mother you'll always receive the heavenly blessings from the above, and you'll always get success, happiness, prosperity and peace in your life.

At your mother's feet there lies a kingdom of heaven.

You'll never pay back what your mother has bestowed you in your life. Your mother is the first guru of your life who introduces you to Almighty God.

Loving your mother means loving yourself, and loving your creator.

Almighty God couldn't take birth in the human form in this mortal world to take care of you every day, but through your mother He comes in your life in order to take care of you.

Love is the mother of everything.

Without love, you're orphan in your life and in your world.

---***---

Love is the mother of everything,

It never asks anything from us.

It only enriches our life.

When it follows in our life

Everything follows in our life-sacrifice,
compassion, happiness, unity

And peace.

Love is the true identity of our life.

Once we forget it everything will be halted in our
life.

Because love is the soul of our life.

Where there is love, there is life and there is
world.

Love never understands hatred;

Love only understands love.

It's only the house of love that we all live together.

No bond in the world will cement us in one
platform,

But it's only the bond of love that brings us under
one roof.

There is only one way to lead a noble life,

And that's the way of love.

18

---***---

Great thoughts to ponder:

We are born of love; love is our mother.

There is nothing as powerful as a mother's love and nothing as healing as a child's soul.

If you want to change the world, go home and love your family.

---Mother Teresa

Motherhood: All love begins and ends there.

A man loves his sweethearts the most; his wife the best, but his mother the longest.

---Irish Proverb

The loveliest masterpiece of the heart of God is the love of a mother.

---Therese of Lisieux

Youth fades; love droops; the leaves of friendship fall. A mother's secret love outlives them all.

---Oliver Wendell Holmes Sr.

---***---

Love is the mother of everything. When she put her footsteps in your life, then everything will be followed in your world.

~~***~~

3. A Divine Love

You never become like god or goddess in this world or on this earth. But you can become like god or goddess with your divine love.

Divine love means complete devotion towards your loving ones or dear ones, where there is no wearing of any kind of mask or playing any drama or pretending of love.

Divine love means your true love, a genuine love to your beloved ones or dear ones, where there is no corruption or adulteration of love.

Divine love means to love yourself and to love your beloved ones or dear ones with heart and soul. Divine love means to love every living creature of this world without any condition.

A divine love means unconditional love.

If you ever give any condition in your life or if you ever try to force any condition on your beloved ones or dear ones, then it means you do not love yourself or you hate your beloved ones or dear ones. Putting condition on anybody means you're trying to compel him to become your slave.

If you ever do so, then you'll never get happiness and peace in your life or in your family. You'll always get unhappiness and uproar.

Many relations and many families are broken up not because they have lack of love, but because of keeping promises and conditions.

You never love anyone with promises and conditions.

You never make any relation with promises and conditions.

You never build a family with promises and conditions.

Promises and conditions are always fatal if you wouldn't fulfill it.

In true love there is no master and no slave.

 In true love there are no promises and no conditions.

In true love there is always a divine love between two lovers.

If you want happiness and peace in your life, then do everything without any condition or obligation, with your open-heart, mind and soul.

Your life always wants unconditional love from you. You never do or receive anything if you make promises and conditions in your life. Making condition means you're forcing yourself and tying yourself in the shackles of obligations.

It is only your divine love or unconditional love which can untie you from the shackles of obligations.

When a devotee goes to offer his prayer in the Temple or Mosque or Church or any other holy places, at that time if he has empty-handed, but if he has a divine heart and a divine love within him, then Almighty God will always please with him, and instantly shower His heavenly grace and blessings to him.

With your divine heart and divine love you will connect with Almighty God.

Your divine love is itself a prayer.

A divine love is the only ladder to reach to Almighty God.

In your life, if you've a divine heart and a divine love, then you can please anybody. You can make your family happy and prosperous.

You can mend every broken relationship. You can build a bridge of love between two divided individuals.

With your divine heart and divine love you can melt everybody's heart, mind and soul.

Your divine heart and divine love are the only source to make your family life happy and complete.

Have you ever asked your parents and your beloved ones or dear ones, what exactly they wish the most important thing in their lives from you, your divine love or materialist needs?

No!

Then ask them once.

You'll get all your answers.

When you make your heart divine, and fill it with your divine love, everything will appear beautiful and heavenly.

You don't need to go anywhere in search of true happiness and peace. You'll get your true happiness and peace within you.

It is your divine heart and divine love which will change your life and change your world.

Your love is the biggest asset, and the most important priority in your life.

Make your heart divine, and fill it with your divine love.

Your divine love is the ultimate source of your lasting happiness and peace in your life and in your world.

---***---

It blooms in the core of our pious heart,

It is the mother of our birth.

Nobody can measure it,

Which we inherit it.

It is the greatest treasure,

Which gives us eternal pleasure.

It makes our life Eden;

It makes our world heaven.

It is a divine love which makes everything pious;

It is the most valuable gift bestowed by Almighty
God to us.

So let's give our pious love to every living being,

And turn them into a heavenly being.

___***___

Great thoughts to ponder:

You are a creature of Divine Love connected at all times to source. Divine Love is when you see God in everyone and everything you encounter.

---Wayne Dyer

Love a man, even in his sin, for that love is a likeness of the divine love, and is the summit of love on earth.

---Fyodor Dostoyevsky(Russian Novelist)

Loving does not about want the other person to be yours; it is about wanting the other person to be happy.

---Vadim Kotelnikov

To live and let live, without clamor for distinction or recognition; to wait on divine love; to write truth first on the tablet of one's own heart- this is the sanity and perfection of living.

---Mary Baker Eddy

All loves are a bridge to Divine love. Yet, those who have not had a taste of it do not know!

Remember that you were born with a divine purpose and destiny that only you can fulfill. Be your authentic self if you want to fulfill that dream that sleeps within your soul.

---***---

~~***~~

*Your divine heart and divine love are the only
source to make your family life happy and complete.*

~~***~~

4. Relation of eternal love

The biggest and greatest relation of your life is only your eternal love. And all other relationships are just for time being, not reliable, and brief. Your eternal love is your everlasting relationship in this world.

Your eternal love is the true identity of your happy and peaceful life.

In eternal love there are no promises or any kind of compliance. In eternal love there is only love and affection. There are no conditions and demands from each other. There is only one and united. Knot and tight. One family. Like a flower and its fragrance. Like two soul mates, two bodies dwelling in one soul.

If there is no eternal love in your relationships, then it'll soon break up into thousands of pieces like a broken glass which you couldn't rejoin or assemble it.

Without eternal love you couldn't think or imagine building any relation in your life. Without eternal love your life is meaningless.

Eternal love is the first foundation of your strong relationship with your beloved ones or dear ones.

Eternal love is cemented forever. There are no break-ups and no hiccups. It'll everlasting both in happiness and sorrows; success and failures; rising and falling. It'll always remain together in every harsh season of life. It'll always remain intact in every tough situation of life. It'll always stand firmly and united in every juncture of life. And nobody could ever dare to shake it or remove it.

There is a great power in eternal love. No external forces of doubts and suspicious could ever separate it or detach it from its relationships.

Eternal love means a firm believed on each other, no matter whatsoever happen in life, alive or death, happiness or sorrow, success or failure.

In other words, eternal love is always united or immortal. It is like an unbreakable string.

Your relationships with your mother and father are always eternal because you're half part of them. It is the fact that you couldn't deny it in your entire life span. And you too couldn't declare that you're not born from them, either. This is the truth of eternal love and eternal relationship.

Eternal love is like the relationship between mother and son.

Eternal love is like the relationship between the tree and fruits.

Eternal love is like the relationship between the bird and wings.

Eternal love is like the relationship between the sun and rays.

If you want to make your family strong and intact, and bind in one string, then always maintain your eternal love amongst the family members in every phase of your life whether in happiness or sorrows; success or failure. Every time.

Always remember that, without eternal love you couldn't build any relation in your life. Without eternal love you'll always find yourself alone and secluded.

It is only eternal love which brings everyone in one union.

If there is no eternity in your love, there is no relationship in your life.

Without eternal love your life is impossible.

Without eternal love your world is under the shadows of darkness.

Every happy and prosperous family always demands eternal love amongst their family members.

Eternal love and eternal relationship are the best gift of Almighty God. Always keep this Abode gift very close to your life.

Make your love eternal and build your relation with eternal love. You'll ever gain eternal happiness and eternal peace in your life and in your world.

Only your eternal love brings mutual respect, mutual understanding, faith and unity in your family.

Only your eternal love can make your relationships with your beloved ones or dear ones perfect and everlasting.

Only your eternal love can make your life complete in this world.

---***---

It's a relation

Which is not tie and knot.

It's a relation

Which is not broken or divide.

But it's a relation

Which bind the whole world.

But it's the relation

Which unite the whole universe.

It's a relation of the whole creation,

Which is heavenly,

Which is divinely.

It's a relation of one heart to another heart.

It's a relation of one soul to another soul.

It's a relation of LOVE

Which is real and eternal.

---***---

Great thoughts to ponder:

Love is a meeting of two souls, fully accepting the dark and the light within each other bound by the courage to grow through struggle into bliss.

True love is eternal, infinite, and always like itself. It is equal and pure, without violent demonstrations: it is seen with white hairs and is always young in the heart.

---Honore de Balzac

Eternal truth, eternal righteousness, eternal love, these only can triumph, for these only can endure.

---Joseph Barber Lightfoot

Love is a symbol of eternity. It wipes out all sense of time, destroying all memory of a begging and all fear of an end.

Through 'Thick and thin'- not 'sick or sin' sharing the goods and bads…….sharing eternal love as long as we live…….

Hatred does not cease by hatred, but only by love; this is the eternal rule.

---Buddha

__***__

~~***~~

Eternal love is the first foundation of your strong relationship with your beloved ones or dear ones.

~~***~~

5. Love blooms everywhere

If you unlock the eyes of your heart, mind and soul, you'll always see the beautiful picturesque of love everywhere. There is no place in this entire world or universe where you won't see or find love. You'll feel its beauty and sweet fragrance everywhere.

Love is universal. Love is everywhere.

Love is the only flower which is blooming everywhere. You'll see it here, there, and everywhere; you'll find it here, there, and everywhere; you'll feel here, there, and everywhere, but only you've to unbolt your veil covered heart, mind and soul.

Once you reveal your clouded heart, mind and soul, you'll see or find or feel your blooming flower of love very close to you. You don't need to search it elsewhere. You'll discover your love very close to your heart.

Your heart is the source of your infinite love.

Your love is always blooming around you like the flowers.

You'll see love on the smiling face of a baby; you'll see love in the blooming flowers; you'll see love in the growing plants and trees; you'll see love in the hovering butterflies; you'll see love in the flying birds; you'll see love in the grazing animals; you'll see love in the flowing river. You'll see love in everywhere and in everything.

Love is the only language which is understood by every living creature in this world. Everybody is the hunger of love. If you ever ask someone with your tender love, in return he will reply with the same tender voice of love.

Love is always giving and receiving.

If you'll give love; you'll always receive it more in return.

If you've a pet dog in your house, then you would know how much your pet dog loves you, and in return how much you too love him. Even a stick which you hold, it too turned into a loving stick for your pet dog.

Never search love elsewhere, it is always stupidity, always search it within you. Your love is like a beating heart which you couldn't halt or separate it from your body. You'll get a hundred percent loves within you. But first of all you've to search it within you rather than seeking it blindly in the outside world. You'll get nothing.

You'll feel love in your every breath, and in every emotion.

Look at your beloved's eyes; look at your dear one's smiles; look at your mother's caring; look at your father's warm hugs; look at your brother and sister's faces; look at your best friend's touch, you'll always feel their undying and unconditional love.

Love is like a growing flower, the more you grow it, the more it grows. Water it every day. Manure it regularly. Look after it day in and day out. One day it'll shower you with its beautiful flower and sweet fragrance of love around you.

Love is the only flower which you can grow in every season of your life. Love is evergreen. It'll never get dry or wet or wilt. It'll ever remain as it is. It'll remain untouched until you won't touch it with your true heart.

Give your undying and unconditional love and affections to your beloved ones or dear ones every day, they will bestow you more than enough love, what you won't expect in your entire life. They are not the hunger of any other things in this world, but they are the hunger of your unending and true love.

Everybody is the hunger of love.

Only your undying and unconditional love impels the hearts of everybody.

It is only your love which rewards you respect, faith, understanding, fellow feeling, humility, generosity, kindness, happiness, and peace in your life and in your family.

If you want to transform your life and your world; then always try to nurture the flower of love in your heart, one day you'll receive its beautiful and sweet fragrance with the beautiful garland of happiness and peace.

Love is the only secret of your lasting happiness and peace. Cultivate it in your life and in your world.

You're a gardener of your life. Everything depends on you; it is up to you which flower you would like to grow in your garden. Choice is yours. Only your choice matters in your life.

But if you ever fail to grow the flowers of love in your garden of world; you'll always find yourself under the thorns of hatred, and under the weeds of anger and jealousy.

Love is the only flower of your life which you can grow and cultivate in your garden of life.

---***---

Love blooms everywhere,

If you want,

You can change this world.

With the worship of love,

You can triumph the whole universe.

With the bouquet of love,

You can turn this Earth into heaven.

With the flowers of love,

You can win the hearts' of this world,

With the language of love,

You can unite the people of this world.

With the bond of love,

You can establish the land of peace.

With the fruits of love,

You can feed the hungers of this world.

Love is the only flower which blooms everywhere.

It's the only seed which you can sow everywhere,

Even it can bloom in the heart of hard rock.

---***---

Great thoughts to ponder:

When you plant a seed of love, it is you that blossom.

---Ma Jaya Sati Bhagavati

True love blooms when we care more about another person than we care about ourselves.

---Elder Jeffrey R. Holland

Life without love is like a tree without blossoms or fruit.

---Khalil Gibran

Happiness blossoms wherever one plants seeds of love and kindness in the hearts of others.

---Melanie Koulouris

Surround yourself with people who allow you to blossom.

---***---

Your heart is the source of your infinite love.

Your love is always blooming around you like the flowers.

~~***~~

6. *Sow a seeds of love*

It's a well said that 'As you sow as you reap'. So, as you sow seeds of love as you reap its everlasting love in your life.

If you ever sow seeds of hatred, you'll always reap its hatred in return.

Love always gives you love.

Hatred always gives you hatred.

It is like tit-for-tat.

As you treat it as it treats you.

Love and hatred never dwell together. If there is love there is no hatred, if there is hatred there is no love.

You could win hatred with love. But you couldn't win love with hatred.

Love means divinity. Where there is love, there is always God's dwelling.

 Love always guides you towards the road of happiness and peace.

On the other hand, hatred means sin or impurity. Where there is hatred, there is always devil's shelter.

Hatred always guides you towards the road of unhappiness and chaos.

Love means alive. Hatred means death.

What do you want in your life?

Love or hatred.

Choice is always yours. If you chose love, you'll live your life in the heaven like world. But if you chose hatred, you'll live your life in the hell like world.

In a land of sandy, dry, rocky, and barren soil, no seeds of any healthy plant ever sow or grow on it no matter how much one could try to yield on it.

On the other hand, in a land of smooth, wet, porous and fertile soil, whatever seeds may be sowed or grow on it, everything grows very well and easily.

Your heart is like a land of smooth, wet, porous and fertile soil.

Never ever try to turn your heart into a land of sandy, dry, rocky, and barren soil.

Many people keep a burning hatred, angers, jealousies, greed, and egos in their hearts, so no seeds of love ever sow in their hearts no matter how hard one could try to yield, and to bring love, happiness, humilities, kindness, generosities and peace in their lives. Everything becomes meaningless.

Enrich your life with the seeds of love, happiness, humilities, kindness, generosities and peace.

If you sow the seeds of love in your life, you'll always reap love. It is like tit for tat. Action and reaction. But if you sow the seeds of hatred in your life, you'll always reap hatred.

It's exactly like if you sow seeds of fruit, you'll get fruits, and on the other hand, if you sow seeds of weed, you'll always get weeds.

You might happen to heard many real incidents that once a woman hates her man bitterly, and then after many years, the same woman starts loving her man very dearly.

How did that happen? Was there any miracle?

No!

The biggest miracle is only love, which can transform anybody. No doubt, initially it seems quite impossible, but with time everything will be changed.

Love can change everybody. Love can change everything.

 Love can do anything.

Love can do miracle.

Here, the most significant point is that, first of all, someone has to sow seeds of love in the hearts of another, then only with the seasons of time, it'll sprout into seedlings of love, and then one day it'll grow into a full-grown plant or tree of love.

Sow seeds of love in your life every day so that you would reap its beauty and sweetness every day; so that you would transform your life like an Eden of love; so that you would make your world into a heaven.

Only love can transform your world into heaven.

In this mortal world, you won't get heavenly life, but with your love you would make your life like a heaven. But it's always depend upon you.

If you wish or want the everlasting happiness and peace in your life and in your world, then you've to sow seeds of love in everybody's heart. When you try yourself, then only the others will respond you later, but your foremost obligation is to sow seeds of love from the very beginning.

There is no other thing in this world which makes you a complete man. But it is only through love, which makes you a complete man.

If there is love, there is life, and there is world.

No love, no life, and no world.

Without love your life is meaningless. Without love your world is void, a complete darkness and hollow, like a Black Hole.

Remember, sowing seeds of love in your life means you're helping yourself and other people. That means you're making this world a better place to live.

Always sow seeds of love so that you could make your life beautiful and pleasant.

---***---

Sow a seed of love

In your heart.

Its sprouting green seedlings

Ever give you a hope of love.

Nurture it…..

Its growing stem

Ever give you a smile of love.

Look after it…..

Its spreading branches

Ever give you a pleasure of love,

Watch it…..

Its dancing green leaves

Ever give you a joy of love,

Feel it…..

Its blooming beautiful flowers

Ever give you a fragrance of love,

Smell it…..

Its bearing juicy fruits

Ever give you a treasure of love,

Taste it....

Sow a seed of love

In your heart

It'll ever give you eternal bliss.

---***---

Great thoughts to ponder:

Sow seeds of love and grow rich!

Sow a seed and let it grow, you never know where love will grow.

---Reed Kroloff

Plant seeds of love, water them with positive thoughts, forgiveness and courage and feel your soul bloom.

Plant the seeds of love in your hearts. Let them grow into trees of service and shower the sweet fruit of Ananda(Bliss). Share the Ananda(Bliss) with all. That is the proper way to celebrate the birthday.

---Sri Satya Sai Baba

If you want to win hearts, sow the seeds of love. If you want heaven, stop scattering thorns on the road.

---Rumi

The heart is like a garden. It can grow compassion or fear, resentment or love. What seeds will you plant there?

---Buddha

When you plant a seeds of love, it is you that blossom.

49

___***___

~~***~~

Enrich your life with the seeds of love, happiness, humilities, kindness, generosities and peace.

~~***~~

7. Love is a part of your life

Think for a second that you've to live your life without love. How do you feel? Can you think a life without love? Can you ever imagine like this? No! You never think or imagine your life without love. If anybody ever thinks so; he is either death or evil spirit or satan.

Love is a part of your life. Without love your life is impossible. Without love your life is meaningless and purposeless. Without love your life is directionless.

It is only love which makes your life possible. It is only love which makes your life meaningful and purposeful. It is only love which guides your life to the right direction, and introduces you the beauties and wonders of this world.

It is only love which gives you new hopes. It is only love which shows you big dreams and high ambitions. It is only love which instigates you to visualize your great visions. It is only love which inspires you to do something great in your life.

It is only love which binds your life and your relationships in one yarn, and leads you throughout your life, and fulfills the purpose of your life.

Love is food of every moment of your life. The moment love goes out from your life, the very moment everything will be split, and you'll find yourself all alone, and you'll die, both morally and emotionally.

In order words, love is your life giving oxygen, without it, it is impossible to think or reflect about your life in this world.

Everything is meaningless without love.

Love is a soul of your life. You can't separate it from your life.

If the roots of a grown up tree is cut down all of a sudden, then automatically the tree will die right way. In the similar way, if your love is cut down from your life, your life will die at once.

Love is a blood of your life. Without it you can't survive for a second.

Love is like a root of your life, without it your life-tree wouldn't survive. If there is a root like love, there is firmness in your life-tree. It'll always hold your life-tree rigidly in every harsh situation; and make your life-tree evergreen. But once it will cut down relentlessly, your life-tree will fall down, and die instantly.

The foundation of every happy and prosperous family is only build with mutual love. If there is a mutual love and affections amongst the family members, there is always happiness and peace prevail.

A family is like a tree which will only grow strongly and healthy with the help of mutual love amongst the family members.

On the contrary, if there is a lack of mutual love and affections amongst the family members; there is always chaos and unhappiness dwell in the whole family.

Love is a breath of your life. Without it your life will suffocate wherever you go or wherever you live.

Love is like the four wheels of a motor vehicle. If there is no complimentary of love amongst the four wheels of a motor vehicle, it'll choke down, and meet with a terrible break down sooner or later.

In the same way, if there is no complimentary of love amongst your dear ones or beloved ones; there will be deteriorating relationships in your family forever.

Remember, no materialistic means ever buy you a complete happiness and peace in your life.

It is one and only your love which brings you a complete happiness and peace, and connects your entire family members in one solid bond.

In the absence of love, your life will become sick and weak. It is only love which would cure your life well and strong.

Love is the only medicine which can heal every emotional illness of your life.

Many relationships break up or fail in the half-way of life, couldn't continue till the end. This is only happened because of lack of mutual love, mutual respect, and mutual understanding with each other.

If there is love, there is always mutual respect, and there is mutual understanding.

If there is lack of love, there is always disrespect, and there is misunderstanding.

Love can build your life. Love can break your life.

Love can construct your world. Love can destroy your world

Love is the only foundation of your life.

Love is the only bridge which connects the two different individuals.

Love is the only ingredient of a long run relationship.

Love yourself. Love your beloved ones. Love every creature of this world.

Love is the only way to live in this world. Love is the true message to live in this world with mutual brotherhood and peace.

Be a part of love. Never depart from love, no matter whatsoever happen in your life. Because love is the most important part of your life.

Without love you're nothing. With love, you're everything. You never detach yourself from love.

Love is a breathing organ of your life.

You're alive because of love.

Love is your part. Love is your life. Love is your world.

Love is within you.

Without love, you're nothing.

Love never demands anything from you.

It simply demands love from you in return.

Only love can change you. Only love can transform you.

Only love can make you great.

Only love can make you a complete man.

Only love can make this world a better place.

Love is the only way to live in this world with happiness, and peace.

___***___

Love is a part of our life,

We can't depart from it.

It's a driving force of our living,

Without it we can't breathe,

Our life will start suffocate.

Without love our life is death.

It's like a body having no heart....

A living corpse.

With love our life gets a new hope,

With love our world gets new life.

Without love our life is lifeless,

Without love our life is meaningless.

Without love,

There will be nothing in our life.

Only the darkness of void will engulf in our life.

In every moment of our life,

It's only love that inspires us to live.

Love is the soul of our life,

That gives the true identity of our life,

And gives us a new light to live our life.

---***---

Great thoughts to ponder:

Love is not finding someone to live with. It's finding someone you can't live without.

Don't find love, let love find you. That's why it's called falling in love because you don't force yourself to fall, you just fall.

Be in love with your life. Every minute of it.

---Jack Kerouac

Love yourself first, because that's who you'll be spending the rest of your life with.

Learn to love with all your heart and accept the faults of others in your life. Remember, anyone can love a rose but it takes a great heart to include the thorns.

Only three things can change our lives dreams, suffering and love.

---Paulo Coelho

---***---

~~***~~

Love is like a root of your life, without it your life-tree wouldn't survive. If there is a root like love, there is firmness in your life-tree.

~~***~~

8. Love is a word of life

Love is a word of only four letters, L-O-V-E. But it is one of the sweetest words in the entire world. Love is a word of life. Love is a word of this world. Love is a word of universe. Love is the mother of every word. Love is the word of eternity. Love is a word of Almighty God.

Love is the sweetest word in the entire world which you never compare with anything. It always sounds sweet and magical. It is always incomparable.

Love makes your life. Love makes your world. Everything is made by love. Love is universal. Love is creation.

Almighty God has created the whole cosmos with love.

No love, no life. Nothing.

No love, no world. No creations.

Without a word of love there is no life; without a word of love there is no world; without a word of love there is nothing. Without a word of love there will be complete emptiness, darkness and silence in this world.

Pass a word of love as much as you could. There is no other magical word like love in the entire world.

You can make anybody as yours with the charms of love.

A word of love is enough to quench the thirst of a man.

A word of love is enough to feed the hunger of a man.

A word of love is enough to soothe the anger of a man.

A word of love is enough to kindle a deserted man.

Love is only a word which doesn't need any explanation.

Love explains itself.

Love is only a word which tells us everything.

Love can mend anything in this world. Love can build a foundation of every relationship. Love can construct a bridge of true friendship between two unknown strangers.

Love brings togetherness. Love brings unity.

Love is not just a word but it is your life. It is your world.

Love bestows you happiness.

Love blesses you peace.

Love is a powerful word.

It can change anybody. It can transform anybody. It's like a magic wane. It can enchant anybody. It can even melt a man of stone heart.

It is a word of love which makes you smile or makes you weep.

A word of love is like an oasis in the desert land.

A word of love is like a drizzle in summer.

There is a great power in love.

There is a great healing power in love.

You may not win any battle with your skills and strengths. But with the power of love, you may win every battle of your life.

Love can make impossible to possible.

Love is your strength. Love is your energy. Love is your power. With the power of love you can do anything in your life. Love is the storehouse of your life. Love is the treasure house of your world.

Love is the only medicine which will heal every wound of your life.

Love is the only water which will extinguish every wild like fire of hatred and jealousy of your life.

Love is the only healer of every agony of your life.

With your love, you can work anything in your life. With your love, you can succeed in every field of your life. Love makes you a valiant to face every challenge of your life.

Love makes you dedicated and passionate towards your life.

It is only love which makes you strong and powerful, and helps you to chase the desire goals of your life.

If you love yourself and your work truly, then no force in this entire universe will ever dare to knock you down. You'll ever rise up, and come out with flying colors. Nobody could stop you.

Love is only a word which is very dear to Almighty God.

With your love you can bring whatever changes you want in your life.

It is only love which will bring a huge difference not only in your life, but also in other's lives.

There is no other thing like love which can transform anything. You can make your world and the entire world a better place with love.

Love is the only answer of every question of this world.

Love yourself. Love everybody. Love this world. Love every creature of this world.

There is no other great message than love. Love is the only true message of this world.

Spread the sweet messages of love everywhere so that with its fragrance everything becomes beautiful and wonderful in this world.

A word of love is the voice of your true heart.

A word of love is comprehended by every creature.

Never forget it.

A word of love can change your life.

A word of love can change your world.

A word of love is the greatest wealth of your life.

A word of love is a worth of million dollars.

---***---

Love is a strong word,

It's stronger than everything.

A word which can fill the heart of every living being.

Love is only word, understands by all.

Whether an infant or a baby;

Whether birds or beast,

Everybody wants to have it.

Because love is the only valuable gift that nobody wants to loss it.

There is a magical charm in love,

It can mesmerize every living heart.

Love is only a word that draws the heart of every creature
towards it.

Love is a word which doesn't need any expressions,

Since it expresses itself everything.

Love is a word of true heart;

Love is a word of pious soul.

Love is word of life,

Without it nobody can live.

It's only a word of love that can bring a new meaning in
everybody's life.

---***---

Great thoughts to ponder:

Love is just a word until someone comes along and gives it meaning.

If you love someone, tell them because hearts are often broken by words left unspoken.

---Pamela Daranjo

Love is a Verb without action, it is merely a word.

Love isn't just a word. It's what you value of someone and promise to never let go.

The first person who teaches you the meaning of the word 'Love' will also be the first person who teaches you the meaning of the word 'pain'.

Love is only a word, until we decide to let it possess us with all its force. Love is only a word, until someone arrives to give it meaning. Don't give up. Remember, it's always the last key on the key ring that opens the door.

---Paulo Coelho

---***---

~~***~~

Pass a word of love as much as you could. There is no other magical word like love in the entire world.

~~***~~

9. *Power of Love*

It's the power of love that you're living now. It's the power of love that you're living with your parents; it's the power of love that you're living with your spouse; it's the power of love that you're living with your brothers and sisters; and it's the power of love that you're living with your friends and neighbors. It's the power of love that holds and maintains everybody and everything in your life. But the moment you'll lose the gripping power of love from you; you'll lose everybody and everything all of a sudden.

The moment you'll lose your love, you'll lose everything in your life.

You'll remain alone, void, and die alone.

We all live in love; we all live with love.

Love is your strength.

Love is your force.

Love is your might.

Love is your energy.

Love is your faith.

Love is your destiny.

Love is your bond.

Love is your foundation.

Love is your life.

Love is your world.

You never detach yourself from love.

Love is your power.

It's the power of love that holds your relations with your parents, with your beloved, with your relatives, with your friends, with your neighbors, and with your colleagues.

Without love there will be no families, no friends, and no relationships. And a life without families, friends and relationships is meaningless and worthless.

There is a tremendous power in your love. The whole universe is binding and standing now because of love. It's only the power of love that we all are surviving in this world.

Love is the ultimate means of your contentment and tranquility.

You never get so much pleasure and contentment in your life which love gives you.

Love gives you everything.

Without love, you're nothing.

Your love is the biggest gift of your life.

Without the gift of love you can't exist in this world.

The moment you lose it; your life will become meaningless.

The moment you miss it; your world will turn into upside down.

Love is the biggest asset for you in this world.

Even if you're penniless, but you've a gift of love in your heart, then you're the richest man in this world.

But if you're rich and wealthy, but you've no feelings of love in your heart, then you're the poorest man in this world.

It is only love which makes you rich or poor.

The more you distribute the sweetness of love the more it'll multiply and diffuse in your life and in your world.

Love has the greatest power in this world.

It is the power of love which can cross every boundary of your life.

It is the power of love which can measure every distance of your world.

If you fall in love with your beloved, then no matter how far you live away from her; you'll always feel her presence very closed to your heart. It's the power of your love which connects strongly with your beloved even you stay far away from her.

You never estimate the infinite power of love.

Love can make a beast into civilize man.

Love can transform anything.

Love can convert impossible thing into possible thing.

Everything is possible with love.

In a small city, a man was living with his wife and two children. He was a very hard-working man. But he never loved his wife and children. He treated them very badly.

His only loved was drinking wine and gambling. He never paid any good attention to his wife and children. He was always finding flaws in his wife and his children. He cursed his fate, and abused his wife every day, and sometimes he thrashed her harshly.

His poor wife, however, loved him very much. She accepted quietly, despite the fact that her husband didn't love her, obeying everything humbly.

She was a noble and devoted wife. She never grumbled anything against her husband's rude behaviors. In spite of that, she used to pray for her husband's well-being and prosperity.

In the same way, the time was slipping away from days to weeks, from weeks to months, and from months to years. But nothing was changed in her husband's odious behaviors and attitudes. He was a same rude and abusive man. However, his poor wife continued doing her responsibilities of a noble wife towards him.

Then one day, the man was met with a terrible accident, his condition was very severe, and admitted in the hospital. When his wife came to know about her husband's terrible accident; she was almost death; she came rushing along with her two children, weeping.

For six months, consecutively, the man was kept in the hospital for further treatment. During those six months, she took care of her husband day and night, tirelessly, sacrificing everything.

Even she had to work very hard in order to maintain her family, and at the same time she had to arrange money for her husband's long treatment.

The poor woman managed somehow. But, she became very weak, and after some days she fell sick while working hard, and taking care of her husband.

At that time, the man for the first time witnessed his wife's unconditional true love and devotions towards him and his family. He realized his grave mistakes, and repented. Then he was a changed person.

He apologized to his wife, and promised her to become a good husband in the future, but, alas, it was too late for him.

The poor woman died the same day when her husband was released from the hospital.

When a person loves someone truly and unconditionally, he'll become very strong. He can do anything; he can sacrifice anything for his beloved ones or dear ones; he can face every tough situations of his life, even though his beloved ones or dear ones didn't pay the same amount of treatment to him. This is the power of love.

Love makes you strong.

Love makes you to sacrifice.

Love makes you to take every challenge of life.

Love makes you to realize.

Love makes you to think.

Love makes you a complete man.

The power of love is not only implied in human relationships, but also in every field of your life. For instance, if you want to get grand success in your life, then your hard work and dedication are not enough, but you've to love your work like you love your beloved ones or dear ones. When you love your work, then everything is possible for you. Every impossible task becomes like a child's play, easy and simple for you.

Love gives you energy and power in your life.

Love is the powerhouse of everything.

If there is love, there is energy of life.

If there is love, there is power of life.

Love is the only power of your life and your world.

---***---

Love is powerful,

It's a source of life,

Without it nobody could live in this world.

It's only love that cement every relation of life,

Without it everything is just faked.

*Love brings you the entire shinning smile in your
tearful eyes.*

It converts the stone hearted soul

Into soft-hearten soul.

Love is the haven of sweetness,

Gives you all the melodies of life.

Love makes your life beautiful;

Brings you all the joys of life.

Love makes your life colorful;

Turns your life into the world of beauty.

Love guides you close to godliness;

Love gives you the pure gift of virtues.

Love is the ointment of everything;

It heals every wound of your life.

Love is your armor of life

That always shields you from hatred.

It's the power of love

That brings every living creature to oneness.

Love doesn't mean that you only love someone
very much

But its meaning is fellow feelings.

Never forget the charms of love in your life.

Be never the part of hatred;

It'll always give you sorrow.

Be always the part of love;

It'll always give you happiness.

If you've a pure love in your heart,

Then only Almighty will bestow His blessings on
you.

It's only love that shows you the path of
righteousness.

Once you follow the path of love,

You'll get the true worth of your life.

---***---

Great thoughts to ponder:

When the power of love overcomes the love of power the world
will know peace.

---Jimi Hendrix

A heart that reaches out with love; can heal a soul, and change a
life.

---Kiran Shaikh

The power of love and caring can change the world.

---James Austry

The power of love is a curious thing, make one man weep, make
another man sing. Change a hawk to a little white dove, more than a
feeling, that's the power of love.

---Huey Lewis

There is no greater power in the universe than the power of love.
The feeling of love is the highest frequency you can emit. If you could
wrap every thought in love; if you could love everything and everyone,
your life would be transform.

---Rhonda Byrne

---***---

It's the power of love that holds your relations with your parents, with your beloved, with your relatives, with your friends, with your neighbors, and with your colleagues.

~~***~~

10. *Love is like a Prayer*

Love is like a prayer. It is sacred and divine. There is no impurity in love. Love makes you sacred and divine being. Love is the only way to live your life. Love is the true purpose of your life.

True prayer of love is the culmination of true heart and soul.

There is only love and faith.

There is only true emotion and contentment.

There is only bliss and serenity.

True prayer of love is your inner voice.

Sing it every day with your pure heart, mind and soul like you pray Almighty God in your temple or mosque or church, morning and evening. Your life will change. Your world will change.

True prayers of love always touch every heart.

True prayers of love always change every mind.

True prayers of love always soothe every soul.

True prayers of love always transform every life.

True prayers of love always convert every world.

Love is always sweet and pious like a prayer. There is a magical charm in love. It'll change your heart, mind and soul the moment it'll touch you.

Every word of love gives you soothing bliss and peace which you won't get or expect from any other source or thing in this world.

Love sanitizes your wrong doings and errs of life, and directs you to the path of righteousness and truthfulness. If your heart is dwelt with the nectar of love, it'll ever guide you towards the road of divinity and godliness.

If you know how to love yourself and others, then you'll know how to live your life in this world. You'll learn the true art of life and living in this world. You'll able to connect with everybody and everything. And you'll know the true meaning of your life.

If you ever failed do anything good to your beloved ones or dear ones, then try to do one favor to them, that is to pray for their well-being with your true love.

Your true prayer of love is always played a miracle in the lives of your beloved ones or dear ones.

Your true prayer of love is always heard by Almighty God.

Your true prayer of love is the voice of your conscience.

Your true prayer of love is the true emotion of your heart.

Pray for yourself.

Pray for your beloved ones.

Pray for your dear ones.

Pray for your family.

Pray for your friends.

Pray for your neighbors.

Even pray for your foes.

Pray for everyone.

Pray for every living creature in this world.

There is a great power in your prayer.

Fill your life and world with the prayers of love.

Sing it every moment.

Chant it every minute.

Remember it every day.

Make it your daily rituals.

It'll lead you to the door of eternal ecstasy and tranquility.

You can make this world a better place with the prayers of your love.

---***---

Love is like a prayer,

It enriches when we share.

Love is divine worship,

It mends the bond of friendship.

Love is devotion,

That changes our life's notion.

Love is pious,

It binds us.

Love is the only medicine,

That cures all our sins.

Love is the language of our heart,

That brings one heart to another heart.

Nobody can live without it,

Love is the greatest feat.

Love cools down the fire of hatred,

And brings us the rain of sacred.

Love cleanses the dirt of our heart and soul,

And build our house in the blissful world.

---***---

Great thoughts to ponder:

Most men pray for power, the strength to do things. Few people pray for love, the quality to be someone.

---Robert Foster

Nothing proves that you love someone more than mentioning them in your prayers.

Never forget the three powerful resources you always have available to you; love, prayer and forgiveness.

Prayer is talking with God and telling Him you love Him, conversing with God about all the things that are important in life, both large and small, and being assured that He is listening.

---C. Neil Strait

If you love someone pray about it. If it's meant to be God will lead you to them.

Prayer is an act of love; words are not needed. Even if sickness distracts from thoughts, all that is needed is the will to love.

---Saint Teresa of Avila

___***___

~~***~~

True prayer of love is the culmination of true heart and soul.

~~***~~

11. *Love is like Music*

Who doesn't love music? Everybody loves music. There is nobody in this entire world who doesn't love music. Music is like love. Love is like music.

Whenever a sweet and melodious music is played on around us, we just feel thrill and relax, forgetting everything. We feel complete and lost in its flowing sweetness and melodies. We feel something new and refreshing aura in our life and in our world. At that very moment everything seems or appears beautiful, colorful, and heavenly.

Likewise, whenever the music of love is played in our life, we too feel the same experiences of beautiful, colorful and heavenly. We feel animated and enchanted. Our life becomes more beautiful. Our life becomes more colorful. Our world becomes like the wonderland. Everybody becomes our dear ones. Everything comes close to us.

Love is the music of your heart.

Love is the music of your mind.

Love is the music of your soul.

Love is the music of your life.

Love is the music of your world.

Without the music of love your life is silent like a death.

Without the music of love your world is dark like a cave.

It is the music of love which brings you happiness and joy in your life.

It is the music of love which brings you contentment and tranquility in your world.

You've to play your music of love in your life every day. Your life always wants the music of love so that you would understand its true meanings; so that you would feel its sweetness, so that you would share its melodies; so that you would live on its magical charisma.

Before a musician plays on any particular musical instrument, first of all, he learns the music; he understands the music; he feels the music; then finally he starts composing a beautiful and melodious tune on that particular musical instrument.

In the same way, first of all, you should know what love is; you should understand love; you should feel love; then only you would finally able to bestow your love to your beloved ones or dear ones.

Love means understanding, feeling and giving.

The more you understand love, the more you feel love; the more you feel love, the more you give love to the others; the more you give love to the others, the more you receive love in return.

Your life is like an orchestra, if you wouldn't play your music harmoniously, there will be no composition of any music at all, a lethal chaos.

A good music is always playing with harmoniously.

Like a good family is always living with harmoniously.

In the similar way, if there is no harmony amongst your family members, then there will be no happiness and peace in your life, a complete distressed and disturbance.

Only love can bring balance and harmony in your life.

Only love can bring balance and harmony in your world.

Only love can bring balance and harmony in your family.

Only love can bring balance and harmony in your relationships.

In your life, you've to play your music of love with harmonious rhythms, so that there will be no missing codes of mutual love, mutual respect and mutual understanding amongst your family members.

If you're a musician, then your love is the music, and your family members are its codes and nodes. You've to play your music of love very cautiously so that your world of composition would sound sweetly and melodiously.

You're a musician of your own life.

You're a musician of your own world.

Every code and node of your music of love is depended upon you.

Whether you play your music of love with melodious tunes or harsh tunes.

Only you can compose the best music of your love.

Nobody can play the music of your love better than you.

Only you can bring the chorus of togetherness in your family with the music of your love.

Your music of love is the best medicine of your wounded heart, mind and soul.

Without the music of love, your life will be like a barren land, dry and deserted.

Only your music of love brings you a new oasis of life.

Love yourself like you love your most favorite music.

Play it every day and everywhere.

Play for yourself, and play for your beloved ones or dear ones.

Spread the music of your love everywhere.

Let the sweetness and melodies of your love will bring eternal happiness, peace and harmony in everybody's lives.

---***---

Love is like music,

It composes in our heart.

It's sweet,

It's awesome,

Every moment it sings in our heart,

It's silently flowing in our heart,

Its softness touches our heart,

Its songs make us divine,

Its melodies make our life pious,

Its every node fills our heart with bliss,

Its every rhythm gives us the meanings of life,

Love is the universal song,

That sings in everybody's hearts.

With its music no one can live in this universe,

Because love is eternal,

Because love is our integral part,

Without its music our life is colorless,

It's only the music of love that makes our life colorful.

---***---

Great thoughts to ponder:

87

Love is like playing music. First you must learn to play by the rules, and then you must forget the rules and play from your heart.

If music be the food of love, play on.

---William Shakespeare

Of all the music that reached farthest into heaven, it is the beating of a loving heart.

---Hendry Ward Beecher

Music is the only thing that you can love without it breaking your heart.

Music is love in search of a word.

---Sidney Lanier

Music is love, love is music, music is life, and I love my life.

---A. J. McLean

---***---

~~***~~

It is the music of love which brings you contentment and tranquility in your world.

~~***~~

12. Love is like a flower

Love has beautiful colors which you couldn't match with anything. Love has the sweetest fragrance which you couldn't compare with anything. Love is always incomparable. Love is always flawless.

Once the flower of love starts growing in your life, you'll become the most beautiful persons in the entire world.

You'll become the richest persons in the entire world.

You don't need anything.

You don't need to go anywhere.

You'll get everything very close to you.

The fragrance of happiness, joy, compassion, kindness, tranquility and peace will envelop you from everywhere.

Love is a flower of this world which blooms in the heart of every living creature irrespective of any difference, and spread her sweet fragrance everywhere.

Grow a flower of love in your life.

Grow a flower of love in your world.

Nurture it every day.

It'll enrich your life.

It'll build your world.

Love is the only flower which can grow everywhere.

Love is the only flower which can bloom in every season.

Plant a tree of love in your heart, mind and soul, and nurture it every day. It'll bestow you immense pleasure and joy in your life.

Once you would plant a flower of love, you won't need to worry about anything in your life. Your life will fill with the colors of love. Your world will fill with the fragrance of love. You'll start living your life in the world of paradise.

If you ever visit in any garden, then you'll know how you feel the moment you enter inside it. You'll feel like every flower is waiting eagerly for you. You'll feel like every flower is greeting you with their undying love. You'll feel like every flower is blooming for you. You'll feel like the wafting fragrance of flowers is tenderly embracing you. You'll feel like everybody is yours. You'll feel like everything is yours. You'll feel like you're the part of everybody and everything. You'll feel like you're always dwelling there.

Then why don't you plant a flower of love in your life, so that you would feel the beauty and sweet fragrance of love every moment of your life.

Your life is always full of sorrows and hardships, if one is gone, then another one is waiting to give you the next challenge. You've no other way to escape from these hurdles of life. You've to face these hard obstacles of life, no matter whatsoever happens. This is called life. And this is the real nature of life. There is no ending, every moment something is happening, and something is about to follow you. You never quit from it, either. At that juncture, it is only love which fanned you with its sweet fragrance and eases your tired heart, mind and soul.

Love is the only flower which shower you everything you need in your life and in your world.

Grow a flower of love in your house so that you could live your life with love, happiness and peace.

This whole world is like a beautiful garden of Almighty God, and you're a beautiful blooming flower of His creation. He purposely sent you in this world in order to live your life in love, and at the same time to give your love to every living creature of his creations.

Love is the only flower which never fades away with the tides of time.

Love is the only flower which ever gives you smiles and laughter.

It'll enrich your life every day.

It'll grow your life the more it becomes old.

---***---

Love is like a flower

That only blooms in our pure heart.

Its every color is the perspective of seven colors

That brings a smile of love on the face of every living being.

Its every drop of fragrance is the magical potion

That quenches the thirst of all living being.

Love is a flower that only blooms in the heart of
pure soul.

Whenever it blooms in our heart,

It makes us divine,

And leads us to the path of heaven.

With the garland of love,

We can worship.

With the bond of love,

We can please our heavenly Lordship.

It makes our heart pious.

It makes our life precious.

Our life becomes beautiful.

World becomes wonderful.

Everything becomes awesome.

Everything starts blossom.

___***___

Great thoughts to ponder:

A flower cannot blossom without sunshine, and man cannot live without love.

---Max Muller

Love is like a beautiful flower which I may not touch, but whose fragrance makes the garden a place of delight just the same.

Love is like a flower, you've got to let it grow.

---John Lennon

Keep love in your heart. A life without it is like a sunless garden when the flowers are dead.

---Oscar Wilde

Love is the flower of life, and blossoms unexpectedly and without law, and must be plucked where it is found, and enjoyed for the brief hour of its duration.

---D.H. Lawrence

Love is a flower that grows in any soil, works its sweet miracles undaunted by autumn frost or winter snow, blooming fair and fragrant all the year, and blessing those who give and those who receive.

---***---

~~***~~

*Love is the only flower which shower you
everything you need in your life and in your world.*

~~***~~

13. *A life without love is worthless*

A life without love is like the sky without the stars, the moon, and the sun.

A life without love is like a wood without trees.

A life without love is like a river without water.

A life without love is like a flower without fragrance.

A life without love is like a bird without wings.

A life without love is like a building without foundation.

Think for a second, can you cut off your body parts? No. You never commit such a crime against yourself. Likewise, you never cut off yourself from your love, because love is your part of life. Without love, you're useless. Your love is your heart.

Nobody could live without love. Love is the part of your life.

Whoever you right now, and whoever you'll become in the coming days, weeks, months and years, all are because of love. Love is the only reason of your life. Love is the only reason of your world.

You're only because of love. You're made of love. You're living for love. You're working for love. You're doing everything for love.

If there is no love there is nothing in your life and in your world.

Without love your life is meaningless.

Without love your world is worthless.

You've no purpose.

You've no hopes and no dreams.

Your life is like a dark cave.

No lights and no ways.

Without love your life is like a barren land.

No plants and no trees.

Love is the part of your life. Love is the part of your world. You never depart from love. It is only love which gives you the purpose of your life. It's only love which gives you the meaning of your life.

It's only love which binds the unity and integrity of your family members and relationships intact. Where there is no love; there is no family, and no relationships.

The moment you keep away from your love, you'll lose everything in your life. You'll become lonely in this world.

You'll never reach anywhere without love. You're breathing in this world only because of love in your heart. Your love is the guiding principle of your life.

If you assume that your life is a ship, then your love is the sea anchor of your ship which guides you every time wherever you sail your ship.

Your love is the destiny of your life.

Your love is the guiding light of your life.

Your life is made by love.

Your world is built by love.

Love is the foundation of your life and your world.

 You never separate yourself from your love.

---***---

A land without fertility is useless.
Nurture it with manure.

A tree without fruit is fruitless.
Grow it with season.

A flower without fragrance is useless.
Enrich it with nature.

A story without moral is valueless.
Write it with wisdom.

A poem without meaning is meaningless.
Compose it with soul.

A word without truth is lifeless.
Speak it with conscience.

A song without melody is tasteless.

Sing it with heart.

A life without love is worthless.

Live your life with love.

___***___

Great thoughts to ponder:

A life without love in it is like a heap of ashes upon a deserted hearth- with the fire dead, the laughter stilled, and the light extinguished.

Life without love is like a tree without blossoms or fruit.

---Khalil Gibran

Life is really nothing without love and care. Give it to everyone but don't except it back. Because it's a feel not a deal.

A flower cannot blossom without sunshine, and man cannot live without love.

---Max Muller

A life with love will have some thorns, but a life without love will have no roses. To the world, you may be one person, but to one person you may be the world.

---Dr. Seuss

A life without love, no matter how many other things we have, is an empty, meaningless one.

---Leo Buscaglin

---***---

~~***~~

Love is the only reason of your life.

Love is the only reason of your world.

Without love, you'll nothing.

~~***~~

14. A True Love is immortal

A true love is like a flower and its fragrance which is immortal.

A true love is like a mother and her son which is immortal.

A true love is like the sun and its rays which is immortal.

A true love is like the music and its melody which is immortal.

A true love is like the rainbow and its seven colors which is immortal.

A true love is always immortal.

A true love is eternal.

There is no end of true love.

The sands of time are running out from you every second, every minute and every hour. Your life is very short, you've no time on your hands, when and how, and in which form, your life would come to the end, nobody knows, and nobody could ever predict it either. Each day and everyday you're heading towards the end of your life, blindly and unknowingly.

Therefore, whoever you want to love in your life, love him or her now. Don't waste your time. Don't wait for anyone or anybody. Don't wait for any place. Just pour the nectar of your true love now, today. Don't wait for tomorrow. Remember, tomorrow never comes in your life. You're living now, today. This is the ultimate demand of the heading time from you. And make your love immortal.

Later on, you won't get enough time to express your true or immortal love to your beloved ones or dear ones.

Your body is mortal. One day it'll perish on this earth. You'll have to leave this world. Thereafter, you'll never know where you would go whether into the heaven or hell or reborn in this earth. Still, nobody ever witnessed the reality of life after death. It is always remained mystery.

But your true love is immortal. Give it now. Pour it out. Don't hesitate. Don't hide it inside the bottom of your heart as dormant. Emerge it out. Your precious time is by and by slipping out from your hands.

Express it now to your beloved ones or dear ones with the top most of your voice, and declare your immortal love as much as you could.

Why are you waiting for?

Say….

'I LOVE YOU VERY MUCH, DEAR SWEETHEART…………………!'

It is very sure, in fact it is the truth, that you'll have to leave this mortal world one day, but you can give your immortal love to your beloved ones and dear ones for eternity without spending too much of time.

Many people couldn't express their true love to their beloved ones and dear ones at their life span, and die without revealing their true love. And their true love dies along with them. Don't do like them.

Express your true love to your beloved ones and dear ones now and then, every moment and every day.

Expressing your true love means you're living your life again and again.

Love is the most beautiful and precious thing in this entire world.

You may find many materialist things in this world, but it is very rare to find a true love.

Do not act like a miser to give your love. Open your heart, mind and soul, and pour out your true or immortal love. Bestow your true or immortal love to your beloved ones or dear ones so that they would recall your true or immortal love forever when you'll not around in their lives.

Your true love will always remain immortal in their hearts.

It'll always act as their great inspiration to live in this world.

It'll always give them the great meanings of life.

It'll always give them the purpose of life.

Shower your true love to your beloved ones or dear ones like the rainfall of the rainy season.

Everything is mortal in this world.

It is only your true love which is immortal in this world.

---***---

A true love is never be ended
In a day
In a week
In a month
In a year.
But it lasts forever.
A true love can't be measured.
You can't measure it with anything.
Neither with the gold nor with the diamond.
A true love is a symbol of its own purity and serenity.
You can buy anything.
But you can't buy a true love.
Because a true love is a confluence of two eternal souls
which remains immortal.

---***---

Great thoughts to ponder:

True love is eternal, infinite, and always like itself. It is equal and pure, without violent demonstrations: it is seen with white hairs and is always young in the heart.

---Honori de Balzac

Love is our true destiny. We do not find the meaning of life by ourselves alone. We find it with another.

---Thomas Merton

Distance is a test of love. Many will fail for those who can't withstand it, but for those who can, there's only one answer. "TRUE LOVE".

Love is patient, love is kind, and what our love expresses is true. No amount of tragedy can tear, or break the love I have for you.

---Jessica Wheaton

True love stands by each other on good days, and stands even closer on the bad days.

True love does not come by finding the perfect person, true love comes by learning to see an imperfect person, perfectly.

---Jason Jordan

---***---

~~***~~

Expressing your true love means you're living your life again and again.

It is only your true love which is immortal in this world.

~~***~~

About the author:

Birister Sharma is a full time author. He is also an avid reader. He loves reading, writing, and motivation. He has penned down dozens of self-help motivational books and novels so far.

You may contact him @ birister2007@gmail.com